# Rich & Poor in
# Mesopotamia
## Iraq in Ancient Times

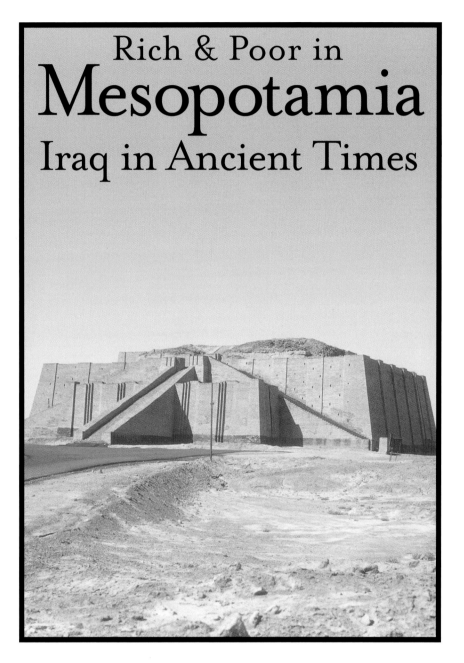

# RICHARD DARGIE

# A+
## Smart Apple Media

First published in 2005 by Franklin Watts
96 Leonard Street, London EC2A 4XD

Franklin Watts Australia
Level 17/207 Kent Street, Sydney NSW 2000

Produced by Arcturus Publishing Ltd.
26/27 Bickels Yard, 151–153 Bermondsey Street, London SE1 3HA

Series concept: Alex Woolf
Editor: Alex Woolf
Designer: Tim Mayer
Illustrator: Adam Hook
Picture researcher: Glass Onion Pictures

Picture Credits:
AKG images: 6 (National Museum, Aleppo, Syria / Erich Lessing), 14 (Musée du Louvre, Paris / Erich
Lessing), 21 (British Museum, London / Erich Lessing), 23 (Musée du Louvre, Paris / Erich Lessing),
26 (Musée du Louvre, Paris / Erich Lessing), 28 (British Museum, London / Erich Lessing).
Art Archive: 8 (Musée du Louvre, Paris / Dagli Orti), 12 (British Museum, London), 13 (Musée du
Louvre, Paris / Dagli Orti), 15 (Deir-ez-Zor Museum, Syria / Dagli Orti [A]), 17 (Musée du Louvre,
Paris / Dagli Orti), 18 (Musée du Louvre, Paris / Dagli Orti), 19 (Musée du Louvre, Paris / Dagli Orti),
22 (British Museum, London / Dagli Orti [A]), 25 (British Museum, London / Dagli Orti).
Bridgeman Art Library: cover and 4, 10, 11 (Musée du Louvre, Paris), 16 (Musée du Louvre, Paris /
Giraudon), 20 (British Museum, London).
Corbis: 7

Published in the United States by Smart Apple Media
2140 Howard Drive West, North Mankato, Minnesota 56003

Library of Congress Cataloging-in-Publication Data

Dargie, Richard.
Mesopotamia / by Richard Dargie.
p. cm. — (Rich and poor in)
Includes index.
Contents: Rich and poor—Houses and homes—Family life—Clothing→Food and feasts—Health and
medicine—Women—Work—Leisure—Country life—The army—Religion—Death and burial.
ISBN 1-58340-723-5
1. Iraq—Civilization—To 634—Juvenile literature. 2. Iraq—Social life and customs—
Juvenile literature. I. Title. II. Series.

DS69.5.D37 2005
935—dc22                                                    2004065300

2 4 6 8 9 7 5 3 1

# ✦ CONTENTS ✦

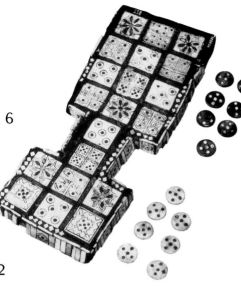

# Kings and Priests

Mesopotamia is the land of two great rivers, the Tigris and the Euphrates, which flow from eastern Turkey to the distant Persian Gulf.

### ❖ LAND OF EMPIRES ❖

Many different city-kingdoms rose and fell in ancient Mesopotamia. The first were in Sumer, close to the sea at Eridu and Ur. By 2000 B.C., the greatest city of Mesopotamia was Babylon, on the banks of the Euphrates. A thousand years later, power and wealth had shifted farther north to Assyria.

The leaders of these cities were kings and priests. The kings held on to power if they were strong in battle and able to protect their people. The priests performed the ceremonies that kept the gods smiling on their city. Another important group of people was the governors and judges who helped run the kingdom.

### SHINING GEM

The Mesopotamian kings were addressed in extravagant ways that reveal something about what people expected their rulers to be like: "Tell my lord the king, the perfect offspring of heaven, our protective angel, the expert and successful warrior, the light among his brothers, the shining gem . . . the provider for scholars, the table laden for all people, Kalbu, who is dust but your favorite slave, sends the following message. . . ."

From a Babylonian clay tablet excavated at Nippur

*The great Ziggurat of Ur was built more than 4,000 years ago and is made from more than 8 million bricks.*

# Common People

After the kings and priests, the next most important citizens were the *awilu*, or gentlemen. They were freemen who owned land and headed large families or clans. They had to help the king raise an army in wartime.

Beneath the awilu were the *muskenu*, or commoners. They often worked as craftsmen or as small traders in the marketplace. Many muskenu worked as servants and cooks in the palace household. Others worked on the farms that were owned by the king.

### ⚜ SLAVES ⚜

The lowest rank were the *wardu*, or slaves. Often they were enemies seized in battle or raids. Most belonged to the king and lived in slave barracks. They were put to work building roads, canals, and other building projects. Some slaves were penniless muskenu who sold themselves—or were sold by their parents—into slavery.

*Most Mesopotamian slaves had hard lives, but some, such as musicians, had special skills that helped them get pleasant jobs in the palace household.*

# Palaces and Gardens

*Most Mesopotamian houses had flat roofs and narrow windows to keep out the hot sun. This clay model, found at Akkad, shows that rich Mesopotamians probably decorated the outside walls of their houses.*

In Mesopotamian cities, the royal palace was built on a high platform so that it looked out over the city. In the center of the palace was the *bitanu*, or audience hall, where the king held court. The palace walls were usually decorated with marble slabs and wall paintings.

Many rich Mesopotamians lived in two-story houses surrounded by a high wall. The houses were built of hard-baked bricks laid on a foundation of cut stone blocks.

Most rooms looked out onto a central courtyard. In the summer, the family used the flat roof as an extra living space and a place to sleep on hot nights. The outside walls of the house were painted white to reflect the intense heat of the sun.

Some wealthy Mesopotamians lived outside the city walls in large houses surrounded by gardens. These houses allowed them to get away from the smells and noises of the crowded city streets.

# Mean Streets

Poor Mesopotamian city dwellers lived in small, one-story houses crowded together in narrow, winding streets. These houses were built using bricks made of mud, strengthened with chopped straw, and then dried in the sun.

## SAFE HOUSES

**Mud brick houses could easily collapse, so a Babylonian law ensured that builders were careful to make them as safe as possible: "If a builder puts up a house but his work is poor and the house collapses and causes the death of the house owner, then that builder shall be put to death."**

From the law code of Hammurabai of Babylon

Most houses had two or three rooms that faced a small courtyard where people could prepare their meals. The windows were covered with clay sheets filled with holes that let in sunlight but were small enough to keep out rats and cockroaches. The doors were painted scarlet, a color believed to be magic, to keep evil spirits away.

### ❧ BEYOND THE CITY ❧

In the marshlands of southern Mesopotamia, poor people made houses from the reeds that grew along the river banks. In the countryside, farm workers lived in simple huts made of intertwined branches covered with a mixture of leaves and dried mud.

*Modern-day Marsh Arabs still live along the banks of the Tigris and Euphrates Rivers in houses made of reeds.*

7

# Lives of Luxury

The father was the most important person in a Mesopotamian family, and he expected obedience from everyone else. On the father's death, the eldest son took over as the leader of the family clan or tribe. It was his duty to make offerings to the household god and tend the family graves beneath the house.

Wealthy Babylonians who had no children often adopted someone as their son. The adopted son agreed to look after his parents when they reached old age, and in return, he inherited their property when they died.

## ✖ MARATHON MARRIAGES ✖

Marriage was important to rich Mesopotamian families because gifts of precious goods such as jewelry, slaves, and land were involved. Arrangements could take months, and the wedding feasts could last for several weeks. Assyrian girls were often married when they were young children, but these child-wives stayed in their father's house until they were mature enough to bear children.

*This 4,000-year-old stone carving from the city of Lagash shows the king leading his people in temple building and feasting.*

# Demons and Debt

Poor families tried to have as many children as possible. Although they were expensive to feed, children could work in the fields or in the family workshop. Sometimes the children of poor families were sold into slavery if their parents fell into debt. In times of famine, parents often gave their children as slaves to the city temple, knowing that the priests would feed them.

Mesopotamian parents feared that evil demons would come and steal the spirit from their children. They sang soft chants or lullabies to quiet their infants because they believed that the demons might be angered by the sound of children crying.

*Children sold as slaves to the temple priests were sure to receive food and shelter. Some were even picked to become priests.*

## Taken into Slavery

A letter surviving from Ur shows how people from poor families could easily become slaves if they owed money to powerful men: "As soon as you left on your trip, Imgur-Sin arrived here and claimed that you owed him one-third of a mina of silver. He took your wife and daughter as pledges for the money. Come back before they die from the work of constantly grinding barley while in detention. Please, get your wife and daughter out of this."

From a wax tablet excavated at Ur

# Classy Colors

*The skill of Sumerian craftsmen can be seen in this elaborate crown of golden beech leaves. It was found in the tomb of Puabi, a royal lady who lived in the city of Ur in about 2450 B.C.*

## FASHION VICTIM

**Mesopotamian youths were aware of the need to look good, as this message from a Babylonian son to his mother shows: "Every year, the clothes of the young gentlemen here become better, but you let my clothes get worse from year to year. At a time when the wool in our house is being used up like bread, you have made me poor, scanty clothes. The son of Adad has two new sets of clothes while you fuss about a single set for me."**

From a Babylonian clay tablet now held in the Louvre, Paris

In most Mesopotamian cities, there were laws about the type and color of clothes that different ranks of people could wear. Kings wore clothes made from cotton imported from India.

Senior government officials wore brightly dyed cloaks to show their status, but the color red was usually reserved for royalty. Another expensive and high-status dye was purple, obtained from shells at Ugarit in Syria.

The Greek writer Herodotus noted that wealthy Babylonian men wore turbans to control their long hair. It was also fashionable to carry a wooden cane bearing a carved symbol such as an eagle or ram.

# Tunics and Kilts

The earliest Mesopotamians wore clothes made from goats' wool. From 3000 B.C., when the Sumerians learned how to weave cloth on a loom, most laboring men wore a tunic made of rough wool. The tunic had half sleeves to leave the arms free for work and was tied with a leather belt.

Men who worked in the open air, such as farm workers, also wore a leather cape. In Assyrian times, most men wore plain linen kilts under long outer robes.

Women usually wore a long dress, and in some Mesopotamian cities, they wore hats in public. Babylonian girls wore a veil, which was removed when they married.

*This stone carving of servants from the palace of King Sargon II shows the long tunics and hairstyles worn by Assyrians.*

### ❧ HAIRSTYLES ❧

To keep cool when working, men cropped their hair short or shaved their heads. Women wore their hair long and decorated it with beads, braids, and ribbons. Slaves had their hair shaved in a special way to show their low rank.

# Gourmets and Gluttons

Wealthy Mesopotamians enjoyed eating foods imported from distant countries. One Assyrian carving shows the king eating bananas from India. Wines were brought from Syria and Lebanon. Wine and fine white cheese were almost always reserved for the kings and high priests.

Several Babylonian recipes have survived on clay tablets. The recipes show that the royal cooks used a wide range of spices, including mint and coriander, to flavor their dishes.

## ✳ ROYAL RATIONS ✳

There was little pastureland in Mesopotamia, so cattle were rare, and beef was expensive. Fattened cattle were given as gifts to the royal and temple households. Another luxury was honey, used to sweeten all kinds of food, including bread.

The kings of Babylon enjoyed cool drinks, so blocks of ice were carried from the highland mountains and stored in deep cellars in the palace.

*This Sumerian mosaic from 2500 B.C. shows the king of Ur and his nobles feasting at a banquet while servants bring food and play the lyre.*

## FREE FEASTS

**During religious festivals, the food in the royal stores was shared at great public feasts: "King Shalmaneser prayed to the gods and lavishly provided them with large cattle and fat sheep. In the shrines of the gods, he offered gifts to everyone. For the people of Babylon, he prepared a feast and gave the freemen gifts of food and wine."**

From the inscriptions of Shalmaneser V on the Balawat Gates

# Daily Bread

*This stone carving from Nineveh shows Assyrian troops cooking and eating in their camp. Assyrian soldiers carried their own supplies with them when they went to war.*

Ordinary Mesopotamians who worked at the royal palace were paid in rations of food. Surviving clay tablets show that palace workers received daily amounts of bread, salt, and beer.

Other workers had to buy their food in the city market or barter with farmers in the surrounding countryside. Beef was very expensive, so the poor ate pork, goat, and horse instead. They could not afford honey, so they used a syrup made from crushed dates to sweeten their food.

Most poor people baked a flatbread made from barley. Bread was also made using rice flour. They ate this with soup made from lentils and chickpeas. In Assyrian times, the poor lived on onion-flavored pancakes. Mesopotamians of all ranks enjoyed snacking on skewered locusts.

In the countryside, people used spears or throwing nets to catch fish from the river. The fish were salted and saved for the winter, when food was scarce. Along the coast, people also ate turtle eggs.

# Medicine and Magic

When wealthy Mesopotamians fell ill, they could call an *asu*. Asus diagnosed illnesses by checking the temperature, pulse, and skin color of the patient. However, they knew little about the body's workings because the study of human corpses was forbidden.

Some doctors performed simple operations such as setting broken bones. This could be dangerous work for a Babylonian surgeon: if he made a mistake, he could have his hand amputated as punishment.

### ◈ DRIVING OUT DEMONS ◈

Wealthy Mesopotamians could also engage an *asipu*, who used magic cures. The most famous asipus lived in the royal palace, protecting the king and his family from the evil demons that were thought to cause illness. They used chants or bribed the demons with gifts.

## SIGNS OF SICKNESS

A set of surviving clay tablets gives this advice to doctors: "If the patient's body and face are yellow, his eyes are yellow, and his skin is flabby, it is jaundice. If a man's face and his body are paralyzed, it is the work of a stroke, and he will die. If he grinds his teeth and his hands and feet shake, it is the hand of the god Sin, and he will die."

From an Assyrian medical treatise excavated at Nineveh

*In Assyria, mysterious healing priests, dressed as* kullulu, *or fishmen, called upon the water god, Ea, to heal the sick and protect the dying.*

# Death and Disease

In Mesopotamian cities, the poor lived packed together in quarters that had little drainage. Food remains and sewage were often thrown into the streets. In these conditions, diseases such as plague and typhus spread quickly. Most poor Mesopotamians died before the age of 50.

Few Mesopotamians could afford a doctor when they fell ill, so they used folk medicines instead. These were made from natural substances such as salt, milk, turtle shells, and snake skin.

The medicines were often dissolved in beer and swallowed. Sometimes they were mixed with boiling water so the patient could inhale the steam vapor. At other times, the medicine was blown into the nose or ear of the patient using a thin, hollow reed.

Some Babylonians used magic charms such as oil, copper, or a dead man's finger. They wore these charms around their necks inside a small goatskin bag.

*Mesopotamian mothers placed images of the wind demon, Pazuzu, beside their newborn children to protect them from disease and death.*

# Wives and Priestesses

## PRAYERS FOR PROTECTION

A priestess describes convent life in a letter to her parents: "At morning and evening, I always pray before the lord and lady gods for your health. I have heard of your illness and am worried. May the lord and lady gods never fail to protect you on the right hand and on the left. Every day at dusk, I pray for you before the image of the Queen of Sippar."

From a Sumerian clay tablet excavated at Sippar

*Women from royal families, such as this Sumerian princess from 2150 B.C., often served as priestesses in the main city temples.*

Mesopotamian women had to obey their fathers and their husbands at all times. Most girls were expected to get married, have children, and look after a home.

When women married, their goods became the property of their husband and his family. However, widows had power over their own lives. They could become head of the family, and some ran businesses as traders or merchants.

### ✖ NUNS IN BUSINESS ✖

Women from rich families could have more control over their lives if they joined a convent and became a priestess or a nun. Nuns were not usually allowed to marry, but they did have privileges, such as keeping the money they made from business. Many bought and sold precious goods such as slaves, silver, oils, and perfumes.

# Women Workers

Poor Mesopotamian women usually did jobs in the home or helped in their husband's workshop. In the countryside, women did the backbreaking tasks of planting and harvesting crops. Others worked as servants in the households of rich Mesopotamians.

Many poor women spun thread and weaved cloth. At the textile workshops in most Mesopotamian towns, up to 40 women worked together, often helped by their children. At Shippurak, women were buried with the stone spindle whorls that they used to make thread.

There were very few jobs that women were allowed to do outside the home. Some ran taverns, and others made a living as midwives. Most Mesopotamian women never learned to read or write, but some did get an education. There were even female scribes in the cities of Mari and Sippar who wrote songs and poems for their masters.

*Weaving cloth was a skilled job that was usually done by women working in the family home.*

# Merchants and Traders

Merchants grew rich by trading in valuable resources such as timber and wine, bringing them from distant lands such as Syria and India. Caravans—long trains of donkeys and camels—carried goods from town to town.

### ✖ SCHOLARLY SCRIBES ✖

Scribes wrote down and read messages and documents for kings and merchants. In Sumer, most scribes came from wealthy families, since it took several years and cost a lot to train a boy to master the alphabet of more than 600 signs.

Many scribes worked for the king, carrying out his orders throughout the kingdom. Others grew rich because they understood the law and could act for merchants in disputes with their customers.

*Sumerian merchants and scribes used wedge-shaped writing called cuneiform to record their business on clay tablets. Many of these tablets, hardened thousands of years ago in the Mesopotamian sun, have survived and can be read by modern scholars.*

### LATE PAYMENT

**Mesopotamian merchants sometimes struggled to obtain their money, as this letter to a customer shows: "We have not received one shekel of money from you. We have sent messages with every caravan . . . but no report from you has ever reached us here. Please deposit the silver for us right away. If not, we will send a notice to the local ruler and the police and will put you to shame in the assembly of merchants."**

From an Assyrian letter discovered in Anatolia

# Craftsmen and Laborers

Craftsmen learned their skills from their fathers or a relative, who took them as an apprentice. Some, such as house builders, had to spend seven years as apprentices before they were allowed to earn their own living. Many joined guilds that set prices for their work and helped them obtain materials from distant parts of the kingdom.

In some Mesopotamian cities, such as Lagash, local people often worked for the temple priests, who owned many of the farms in the kingdom. Others worked for themselves. Families often had a small garden where they grew fruits and vegetables to sell at the market.

*Nangars, or carpenters, were employed to build houses, furniture, and the small boats that traveled the Tigris and Euphrates. They used bronze and copper tools to shape the wood.*

Some of the hardest jobs were done by prisoners of war who were taken as slaves. One Sumerian writer describes prisoners being blinded to keep them from running away. They were treated like beasts of burden and made to dig irrigation ditches in exchange for scraps of food.

# Sport and Study

Assyrian kings spent much of their time hunting fierce animals such as lions. Teams of beaters walked through the long grass, banging drums to scare the animals into running toward the king, who was waiting in his chariot.

The lions were usually killed by his arrows, but sometimes, to show his bravery, the king would approach the animal on foot and kill it with a javelin. Lion hunting was not just a game. If the king was successful in the hunt, it was seen as a sign that he was favored by the gods.

## ❖ SCIENTIFIC LEARNING ❖

Some wealthy Mesopotamians used their free time to study and think. By 3000 B.C., the Sumerians had discovered many rules of mathematics and had invented a system for measuring seconds and minutes based on the number 60. Babylonian astronomers studied the stars. They calculated a calendar of 354 days based on the movement of the moon.

*A royal lion hunt. Beaters on foot clashed their swords and shields to flush lions out of the long grass so that they could be hunted by the king in his chariot.*

# Festivals and Fun

*Sumerian nobles played games of skill and chance on highly decorated game boards such as this one, found in the royal tombs at Ur.*

Important religious festivals were marked by celebrations and banquets in Babylon. At one royal feast in the palace at Calah, there were almost 70,000 guests. The festivities lasted more than 10 days. Entertainment at these banquets was provided by musicians, jugglers, acrobats, and even snake charmers. Men and women danced in honor of the goddess Ishtar. Long poems about the gods and famous battles were sung before the king.

### ⊰ Toys and Games ⊱

Board games and gambling were popular pastimes with Mesopotamians of all ranks. Boards were usually made from clay or soft, carved stone, and the pieces were often named after animals. Children from poor families played with toys such as boomerangs and bows and arrows. Archaeologists have also found spinning tops and rattles in humble Mesopotamian homes.

## Festival Preparations

**A letter from Nineveh shows the elaborate planning behind the festivals at the Assyrian royal palace: "Get everyone together, open the storehouse, and have the chests taken out. Take garments from the chests, as many as you can carry. Also take out 20 pounds of dye, 20 pounds of minerals, 1 jar of perfume, also containers with aromatic spices. . . ."**

From an Assyrian clay tablet discovered at Assur

# Close to the City

**W**ealthy Mesopotamians seldom built large houses for themselves in the countryside. It was very hot in the summer months, and people preferred the coolness of the city's marble palaces and temples to the sun-baked fields of the countryside.

Those who did have homes in the countryside built them close to the city. Wars between the cities of Mesopotamia were common, as were raids by foreign enemies such as the Guti tribes. The countryside could be a dangerous place.

However, many wealthy families owned farms in the countryside that were worked by slaves.

## ✶ TRANSFORMING THE LAND ✶

The strong Assyrian kings took more interest in the countryside. In 700 B.C., Sennacherib made Nineveh his capital city. He moved thousands of people from other parts of his kingdom and made them work at turning the dry countryside around Nineveh into farms, orchards, and parks. A system of canals was built to bring water from the hills to the new capital.

*The gardens around the Assyrian city of Nineveh were watered by the Tigris River and tended by hundreds of gardeners.*

# Canals for the Crops

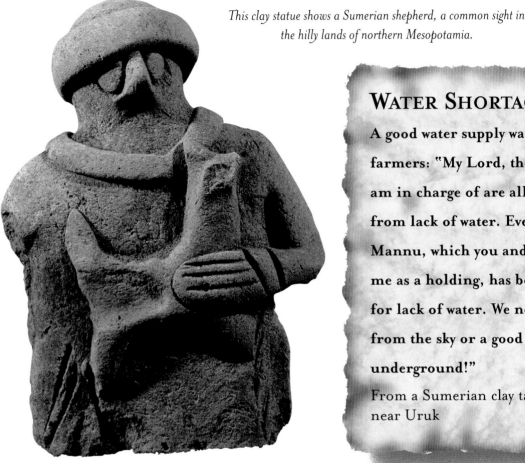

*This clay statue shows a Sumerian shepherd, a common sight in the hilly lands of northern Mesopotamia.*

## WATER SHORTAGE

**A good water supply was vital to farmers: "My Lord, the farms that I am in charge of are all suffering badly from lack of water. Even the town of Mannu, which you and the king gave me as a holding, has been abandoned for lack of water. We need either rain from the sky or a good flood from underground!"**

From a Sumerian clay tablet excavated near Uruk

Many poor Mesopotamians lived in small country villages. Others lived in the cities but left them each day to work in the garden suburbs. Most worked in the fields tending livestock and crops or in the orchards where dates and fruits such as pomegranates were grown.

The royal palace and the great temples employed vast numbers of workers. Sometimes the king ordered laborers to repair the network of canals and ditches that spread water from the rivers to the fields. The main crop was barley, grown in fields that depended on water from these canals. Teams of men and oxen plowed the fertile land.

Some people transported goods from one part of the kingdom to another. They carried the goods on their backs or used pack animals such as donkeys and camels. Many goods were transported by covered wagon or by boat along the rivers.

# Battle and Booty

A Mesopotamian king was expected to lead his armies into battle in his chariot, surrounded by a detachment of *quradu*, his best troops. Victory was a sign that the king enjoyed the favor of the gods. A defeated king was almost always executed.

A victorious king could win a lot of booty. Thousands of prisoners were also taken. Wealthy prisoners could be ransomed, but most ended up as slaves.

## ❈ ENGINEERS ❈

Engineers were important officers in the Assyrian army. They organized the building of roads and bridges when the army was on campaign. They designed siege towers and scaffolds to scale city walls.

*War chariots were first invented in Mesopotamia in about 2500 B.C. and were drawn by teams of wild asses called onagers.*

## WAR STORY

**Assyrian king Sennacherib (705–681 B.C.) recorded his battle against the Babylonians: "Like the onset of a swarm of locusts, the enemy came. . . . I prayed to the gods for victory over the foe. I put on my coat of mail and my helmet and mounted my battle chariot. I seized the mighty bow of Assur and my javelin, and pressed forward toward the enemy host, decimating them with arrow and spear. The bodies of their dead warriors filled the plains like grass."**

From the records of the Eighth Campaign inscribed upon the Sennacherib Prism

# Soldiers of the King

*This carving shows Assyrian troops using ladders to scale the walls of an enemy town and executing prisoners.*

In early Mesopotamian times, men joined the army to fight an enemy and went back to their homes when the battle was over. The first armies of full-time soldiers were in the cities of Akkad. King Sargon (2340–2284 B.C.) led more than 5,400 professional troops.

Most ordinary soldiers fought on foot using spears and swords. The Sumerian infantry wore helmets and armor of thickened leather. There were also detachments of lightly armed archers.

Later Mesopotamian armies used stronger armor and bronze weapons. The Assyrians made most of their armor and weapons from iron, which was harder than bronze and cheap to produce.

## ❧ REWARDS AND BENEFITS ❧

Men who joined the Babylonian army were rewarded with land. They could also win a share of the booty from a defeated city. Serving in the army was a way that men from other regions could show their loyalty to the Mesopotamian kings.

# Priests and Prophets

The king of a Mesopotamian city was also the high priest. It was his job to make offerings to the city's god. To make sure that the god remained friendly, the king had to observe many taboos. These were strict rules about things that he was not allowed to do, such as eat particular foods or wear certain colors of clothes. If the king forgot a taboo, he had to be ritually cleansed.

## ❋ SEEING THE FUTURE ❋

The ruling families of Mesopotamia used priests called diviners to try to predict the future. They believed that the diviner could tell the future by looking at the liver of a sacrificed animal or by studying the movement of the planets in the night sky.

*This clay seal shows a priest praying to Marduk, the most important Babylonian god.*

## FLIGHTS OF FANCY

The Mesopotamians believed they could tell the future by watching birds: "If a raven carries something into a house, the owner will get something that does not belong to him. If a falcon drops something he is carrying upon a person's house . . . this house will have much profit. If a bird carries meat or another bird and drops it upon a person's house, the owner will get a large inheritance."

From a letter to Assyrian King Esarhaddon (seventh century B.C.)

# Gods, Ghosts, and Demons

The Mesopotamians believed in hundreds of gods and goddesses. Every city and village was protected by its own special god. The patron god of Babylon was Marduk, who lived in the great temple of Esagila in the center of the city. Babylonian women prayed to Ishtar, the goddess of love and fertility.

The most important religious festival in Babylon was New Year. The celebration lasted for 12 days. Images of all of the gods of Babylonia were carried through the streets to the temple of Marduk, who was reborn on the first day of the new year.

## ⊲ SPECTRAL SPINSTERS ⊳

Mesopotamians also believed in demons such as the *lilu*, who were the spirits of people who had died unmarried. They entered homes looking for victims to become their spouses in the demon world. Most Mesopotamian homes had images of friendly spirits near their doors to keep demons from getting in.

*Most Mesopotamians believed that the spirits of the dead could come back and haunt them. Professional ghost raisers were sometimes hired to ask the spirits to stop haunting the family.*

27

# Royal Remains

Mesopotamians believed that after death, their spirit went to a dark, grim netherworld. The dead were often buried with things they would need in the spirit world, such as flasks containing food and water.

When the king of Sumer died, treasures such as jewelry, an ivory game board, a harp, and a chariot were put into his tomb. The graves of Prince Meskalamdug and Queen Puabi of Ur were surrounded by the bodies of 5 armed guards and 70 maids holding lyres. Archaeologists believe that these servants were deliberately poisoned so that they could accompany their royal master and mistress to the netherworld.

In Assyrian times, important people were often buried in coffins made of glazed terra cotta and decorated with scenes from the life of the person who had died.

*This golden statue of a ram caught in a thicket was found in the royal tombs of Ur by British archaeologist Sir Leonard Woolley. It is one of the oldest works of art in the world.*

# Family Spirits

When poor Mesopotamians died, they were often buried beneath the family house, usually below a quiet room or directly beneath the thick walls. Bodies were buried in clay coffins or brick boxes. Very poor families simply wrapped the dead in reed matting and placed them in the ground.

In this way, the spirits of the family's ancestors were kept close to the family and could be cared for. It was the duty of the head of the family to offer water to his dead relatives every day by pouring it over their graves.

## LAMENT

Sad songs called laments were sung by friends and relatives at a funeral: "I cry for my friend Enkidu. . . . An evil demon appeared and took him away from me. My dear friend, that swift mule, that fleet wild horse of the mountain, that panther of the wilderness, now what is this sleep that has seized you? You have turned dark and do not hear me."

From *The Epic of Gilgamesh*

## ⚛ GRAVE GOODS ⚛

Pottery bowls containing meat and oil were often put into the grave at the feet of the dead. Sometimes small human and animal figures were also placed there. These grave goods were laid out for several days after the funeral so that friends and family could view them.

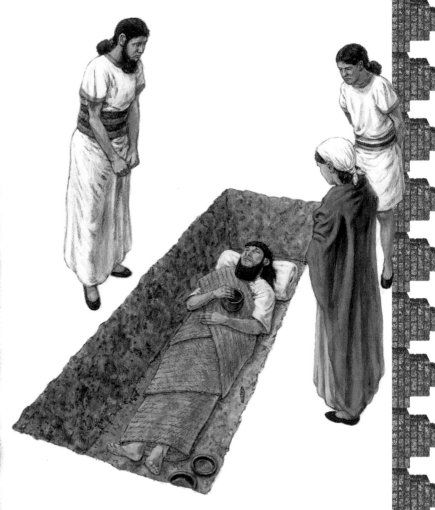

*Most Mesopotamians wanted to be buried in or close to the family home. If they died far from home, they feared that their spirit might roam the world forever.*

**B.C.**

| | |
|---|---|
| c. 4000 | The first large walled towns are built in Mesopotamia. |
| c. 3900 | The earliest use of wheels and writing in Mesopotamia. |
| c. 3000 | Sumerian city-kingdoms of Ur and Lagash are at their peak. |
| c. 3000 | The earliest use of bronze tools and weapons. |
| c. 2800 | The first use of cuneiform writing on clay tablets. |
| c. 2500 | The rise of Akkadian cities such as Sippar and Babylon. |
| c. 2500 | The earliest use of horses. |
| c. 2250 | Sargon of Akkad builds his kingdom. |
| c. 2000 | Babylon becomes the most important city in Mesopotamia. |
| c. 2000 | The earliest use of chariots and spoked wheels. |
| 1792–1750 | The reign of Hammurabai, the lawgiver king of Babylon. |
| c. 1500 | The earliest use of glass and glazed pottery. |
| c. 1400 | The introduction of camels into Mesopotamia. |
| c. 1350 | Assyria becomes the leading power in Mesopotamia. |
| c. 1000 | The first use of metal coinage. |
| c. 700 | Sennacherib builds a new capital city at Nineveh. |
| c. 700 | The introduction of cotton to Mesopotamia. |
| 612 | Nineveh is captured by the Medes and Babylonians. The fall of the Assyrian kingdom. |
| 539 | Babylon is captured by the Persians. The end of independent Mesopotamia. |

**Further Reading**

Klingel, Cynthia, and Robert Noyed. *Ancient Mesopotamia.* Minneapolis: Compass Point Books, 2003.

Malam, John. *Mesopotamia and the Fertile Crescent, 10,000 to 539* B.C. Austin, Tex.: Raintree Steck-Vaughn, 1999.

McCaughrean, Geraldine. *The Epic of Gilgamesh.* Grand Rapids, Mich.: Eerdmans Books for Young Readers, 2003.

Moss, Carol. *Science in Ancient Mesopotamia.* New York: Franklin Watts, 1998.

**Web sites**

http://www.learner.org/exhibits/collapse/mesopotamia.html

http://www.mesopotamia.co.uk/menu.html

http://www.wsu.edu:8080/~dee/MESO/CONTENT1.HTM

**amputate**  Cut off a limb.

**apprentice**  Someone learning a craft or trade.

**astronomer**  Someone who studies the night skies.

**booty**  Valuable goods taken from a defeated enemy.

**bronze**  A shiny metal made from copper and tin.

**caravan**  A group of merchants traveling together for safety.

**chickpeas**  Large, edible peas, originally from Persia.

**cockroach**  A large, black beetle that lives in human homes.

**convent**  A home for nuns and priestesses.

**coriander**  A plant whose seeds are used to flavor food.

**courtier**  A trusted attendant of the king.

**dye**  A mineral or vegetable stain used to color cloth.

**guild**  A group of craftsmen from the same trade.

**irrigation**  The process of bringing a supply of water to a dry area in order to help crops to grow.

**javelin**  A short throwing spear.

**linen**  Fine cloth made from river reeds called flax.

**locust**  A crop-eating insect once common in the Middle East.

**loom**  A wooden frame used for weaving thread into cloth.

**lyre**  An ancient musical instrument similar to the harp.

**midwife**  A woman with skill in helping other women give birth.

**omen**  A sign of a good or bad future event.

**pasture**  Grasslands used for feeding animals such as cattle.

**patron**  Someone who gives support or protection to another.

**plague**  A highly infectious and lethal disease.

**plaque**  A small tablet inscribed with words or an image.

**ration**  A small share or portion of food.

**scribe**  An educated secretary able to read and write messages.

**sewage**  Human and domestic waste matter from buildings, especially houses.

**suburbs**  The areas outside the main part of a city.

**turban**  A long piece of cloth wrapped around the head.

**whorl**  A small stone disk used as a wheel when spinning wool.

**typhus**  A dangerous fever spread by lice.

**ziggurat**  An ancient Mesopotamian pyramid-shaped tower with a square base, rising in stories of decreasing size, with a terrace at each story and a temple at the very top.

Page numbers in **bold** refer to illustrations.